Searching for an Optimal Strategy for
Identifying Files to Review for Fair Lending Exams

Jason Dietrich
September, 2005

OCC Economics Working Paper 2005-3

Keywords: Outliers, Logit, Fair Lending

Jason Dietrich is an Economist in the Financial Access and Compliance group at the Office of the Comptroller of the Currency. Please address correspondence to Jason Dietrich, Economist, Risk Analysis Division, Office of the Comptroller of the Currency, 250 E. Street, S.W., Washington, DC 20219 (phone: 202-874-5119; e-mail: jason.dietrich@occ.treas.gov)

Searching for an Optimal Strategy for
Identifying Files to Review for Fair Lending Exams

Jason Dietrich
Office of the Comptroller of the Currency

September 2005

Abstract: A manual review of applications is an important component of statistically modeled fair lending exams. How files to review are identified affect both resource allocation and reliability of conclusions. This study uses Monte Carlo simulation to compare how six outlier identification strategies perform at identifying disadvantaged applicants. The results show that the optimal strategy for minimizing cost and maximizing reliability of conclusions depends on the likelihood and severity of disadvantage. Further, none of the strategies are highly successful at identifying disadvantaged applicants or minimizing the number of non-disadvantaged applicants reviewed.

The views expressed in this paper are those of the author alone, and do not necessarily reflect those of the Office of the Comptroller of the Currency or the Department of the Treasury. The author would like to thank Chau Do, Mike Carhill, Irene Fang, Gary Whalen, Mark Levonian, and Amy Millen for their insightful comments and editorial assistance.

I. Introduction

One objective of a fair lending analysis of mortgage applications is to identify individual applicants who have been disadvantaged. With unlimited resources, a thorough review of each application in the population is optimal. Unfortunately, regulators do not have unlimited resources and face a cost/reliability tradeoff. Reviewing more files increases cost, but also increases the reliability of conclusions drawn. As a result, when identifying applications to review, it is important to use a strategy that maximizes the likelihood of identifying disadvantaged applicants, while minimizing the likelihood of reviewing applicants that are not disadvantaged. Currently, there is no convincing theoretical or empirical evidence identifying one strategy that best accomplishes those goals.

Addressing the cost/reliability tradeoff when choosing files to review has always been important for fair lending analyses, but it is becoming even more important as these analyses begin focusing more on pricing disparities. Historically, fair lending analyses have focused on disparities in underwriting decisions. For these analyses, standard statistical methods have proven effective at identifying systematic patterns of disparate treatment, and consequently indicating the importance of a file review. In the extreme case, one could argue that no file review is necessary if no statistical evidence of disparate treatment exists. Although in practice, some file review is always necessary. The additional information from the statistical analysis makes choices about the cost/reliability tradeoff less important.

Recent changes to the Home Mortgage Disclosure Act (HMDA), requiring lenders to gather and report pricing data, shifts the focus of fair lending analyses from disparities in underwriting to disparities in pricing. Pricing analyses present a number of econometric challenges that make the search for systematic patterns of disparate treatment difficult. As a result, the statistical results provide less information about the importance of a file review, thereby making the file review more important in general. Choices about the cost/reliability tradeoff become more important as well.

This study uses Monte Carlo simulation to compare and contrast six outlier identification strategies for identifying disadvantaged applicants. The six strategies are: 1) absolute residuals, 2) relative residuals, 3) influence statistics (DFBETA), 4) matched pair analysis, 5) forward searching method, and 6) non-parametric tree algorithm. Discrimination is artificially introduced into data from a recent OCC fair lending exam by increasing the APR for a subset of minority applicants. The frequency and magnitude of discrimination, as well as the subset of minority applicants who are disadvantaged, are all varied during the simulation. For each simulated dataset, each of the six outlier identification strategies is used to identify the disadvantaged applicants. Two measures are used to compare the performance of the six strategies: 1) the percentage of disadvantaged applicants found, and 2) the percentage of non-disadvantaged applicants identified. Strategies that identify a high percentage of the disadvantaged applicants while minimizing the number of non-disadvantaged applicants reviewed are preferable.

The remainder of the paper is constructed as follows. Section II provides a brief summary of the research on outlier identification strategies. Section III then describes in detail the six strategies that are analyzed in this study. Section IV discusses the data generating process (DGP) and the Monte Carlo simulation used to compare and contrast the effectiveness of each of strategy. Section V contains the simulation results, and section VI concludes the discussion.

II. Background

This study focuses on identifying individual applicants that were disadvantaged in the price paid for a mortgage. A disadvantaged applicant receives a price that is higher than expected given his risk profile. From a statistical or modeling perspective, applicants with values for the dependent variable (price) that look different than expected are referred to as outliers.[1] Similarly, applicants with values for an independent variable that lie outside the range of the rest of the applicants are categorized as leverage points.

Graph 1 presents a scatterplot of APR and LTV, which shows the differences between outliers and leverage points.[2] The bulk of the data points, labeled (a), are the regular observations that convey the true underlying relationship between APR and LTV. In this case, increases in LTV lead to fairly linear increases in APR. Points (b) and (d) are outliers, because they deviate from the linear pattern formed by points (a). In other words, the price these two applicants paid is different than expected given their LTV values. This study focuses on strategies to identify outliers, such as points (b) and (d). Points (c) and (d) are leverage points, because the LTV values are much larger than the LTV values for the rest of the applicants. Point (d) is therefore both an outlier and a leverage point. Because point (c) does not deviate from the linear pattern formed by the

---

[1] Under OCC policy, OCC examiners look for disadvantage of any size. Therefore, unlike the typical view of outliers, the unexpected differences do not need to be extremely large for an applicant to be deemed an outlier in this study.
[2] This graph is based on a graph presented in Rousseeuw and Zomeren (1990).

data points (a), it is viewed as a good leverage point. Point (d) does not lie on this line and is therefore called a bad leverage point. This study does not analyze leverage points.[3]

Concern about the effects of outliers on statistical estimators, and how to identify them has existed for almost 70 years (Pearson and Sekar, (1936)). Some significant

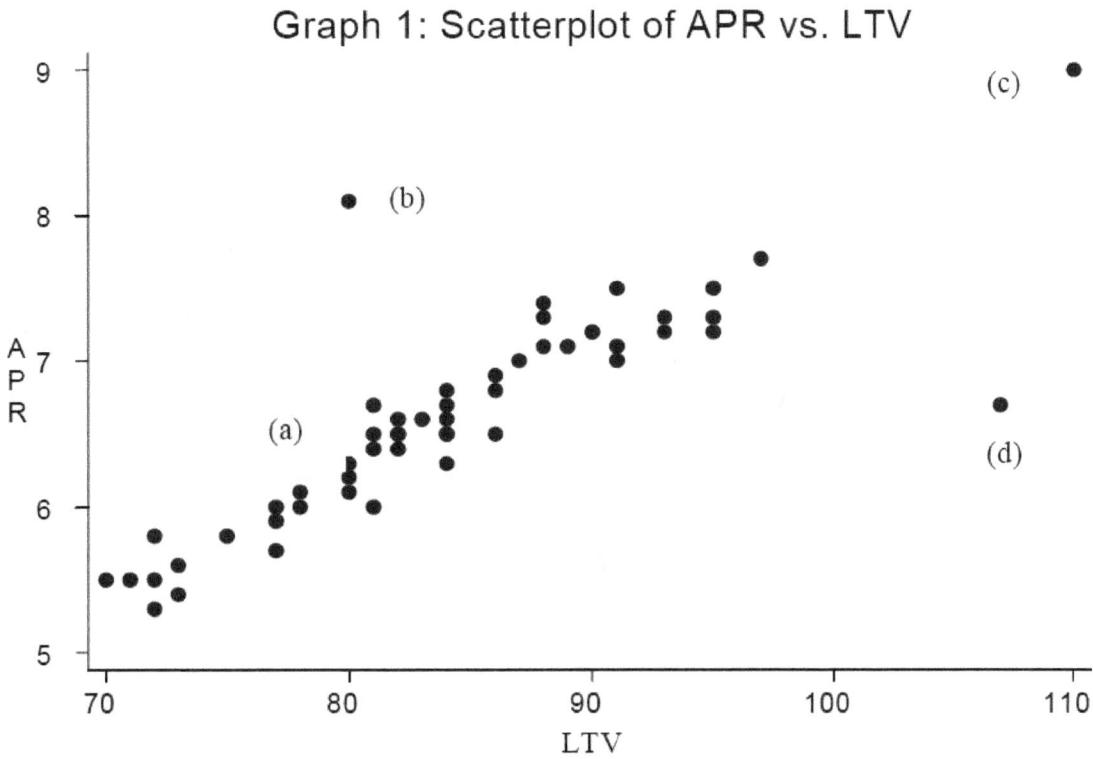

Graph 1: Scatterplot of APR vs. LTV

advances have been made over this time period. For example, the problem of locating a singular outlier in multivariate data has been resolved for more than 20 years (Barnett and Lewis, (1978)). What has not been resolved is how to identify multiple outliers in multivariate data. This task is hindered by two problems, masking and swamping. Masking occurs when an application is an outlier, but is not identified as one by the method being used. In this instance, potentially disadvantaged applicants are not being

---

[3] There is a large literature analyzing leverage points. For more information, see Atkinson (1994), Hadi (1992), Hawkins and Bradu (1984), Maronna and Yohai (1995), and Rock and Woodruff (1996).

identified. Swamping occurs when an application is not an outlier, but is incorrectly identified as an outlier. In this instance, applications are unnecessarily reviewed, which drives up resource costs.

Masking and swamping are typically caused by other nearby outliers. For example, suppose a dataset has no outliers, and that the dependent variable APR is only a function of a constant and LTV. On a scatterplot of APR on LTV, a regression line generally dissects the middle of the data. If an outlier is added to the data, the regression line will rotate or shift, causing some of the original observations to appear now as outliers (swamping). If additional outliers are added close to the original outlier, these outliers may not be picked up as outliers because of the more pronounced rotation or shift of the regression line toward these outliers (masking).

Much of the literature on outlier identification focuses on developing strategies to overcome the problems of masking and swamping. Similarly, this study uses Monte Carlo simulation to determine empirically which of six outlier identification strategies best overcomes masking and swamping in a fair lending context. The overall goal is to identify a strategy that is highly successful at finding truly disadvantaged applicants and minimizing the number of non-disadvantage applicants included in file review samples.

III. Strategies for Identifying Outliers

This section details the six outlier identification strategies that are compared and contrasted in this study: 1) Absolute residuals, 2) Relative residuals, 3) DFBETA, 4) Matched pairs, 5) Forward searching, and 6) Tree algorithm. Each of these strategies is discussed in turn.

1. Absolute Residuals

The first strategy is based on the residuals from a statistical model explaining the price applicants pay for a mortgage.[4] This study uses APR as the measure of price and the OLS estimator to estimate all models. The set of independent variables, along with summary statistics, are presented in Appendix A. Race is never included as an independent variable, because the file review focuses on determining the effects of race. Once a model is estimated, it is used to predict the price each applicant should expect to pay given his or her risk profile. Applicants with larger deviations between actual and predicted price are deemed more likely to be disadvantaged and in need of review. Therefore, the residuals can be used to rank order all applicants from those most likely to be disadvantaged to those least likely. As a result, it is possible to show how this strategy ranks on the two performance measures for file review samples of different sizes.

The first outlier identification strategy is called the absolute approach, because an outlier is defined solely on the deviation of the predicted price from the actual price, and is not based on a comparison of similarly situated applicants. This is the most common strategy used during past statistically modeled fair lending exams conducted by the OCC. The OCC has used this method primarily because this is the standard residual analysis typically conducted when estimating any parametric model.

---

[4] As with all residual-based discrimination analyses, the reliability of this approach depends on accurately predicting the price for each applicant based on his risk profile. If these predictions are not accurate, then a large positive residual may be due to factors other than discrimination.

2. Relative Residuals

Similar to the first outlier identification strategy, the second strategy is based on the residuals from a statistical model explaining the price applicants pay for a mortgage. Price is defined as the APR, OLS is used to estimate all models, and the set of independent variables is the same as for strategy 1. Unlike the first strategy, information about similarly situated applicants is now incorporated. Specifically, each applicant is assigned a comparison group, which consists of all other applicants with a price within +/- 25 basis points.[5] Using the residuals, a relative residual measure is constructed. For a minority applicant the relative residual equals his or her residual value less the largest residual for white applicants in the comparison group. Similarly, for a white applicant, the relative residual measure equals the difference between his or her residual and the largest residual for minority applicants in the comparison group. Applicants with larger values for this new measure are deemed more likely to be disadvantaged and in need of review. Therefore, this measure can be used to rank order all applicants from those most likely to be disadvantaged to those least likely. As a result, it is possible to show how this strategy ranks on the two performance measures for file review samples of different sizes.

APR reflects the risk-based factors and adjustments from the lender's rate sheets, as well as tradeoffs between note rate and fees or points. Therefore, to some extent, two applicants with similar APRs have similar expected returns to the lender. If the statistical model suggests an applicant is over-priced relative to other applicants with similar prices, the APR for that applicant potentially includes a discriminatory premium. Using this

---

[5] Using 25 basis points to define a comparison group is arbitrary, and the results may change if different cutoffs are used.

approach, applicants with smaller residuals may still be identified as potentially disadvantaged if their residuals are large relative to their comparison group. As with the first strategy, the accuracy of the predicted APR values is very important.

3. DFBETAs

The third strategy uses an influence statistic called the DFBETA to define outliers.[6] DFBETA conveys the influence each application has on the coefficient estimates in the model. For purposes here, the coefficient estimate of interest is the race variable. Therefore, unlike the first two strategies, race is now included in each model. Price again is defined as APR, OLS is used to estimate all models, and all of the independent variables listed in Appendix A are included.

For a particular application, DFBETA is the standardized change in the racial coefficient estimate if the model is estimated with that application excluded from the dataset. All else being equal, disadvantaged minority applicants should have a positive effect on the estimated coefficient for the race variable. This is conveyed by large positive values of the DFBETA statistic. Therefore, the DFBETA measure can be used to rank order all applicants from those most likely to be disadvantaged to those least likely. As a result, it is possible to show how this strategy ranks on the two performance measures for file review samples of different sizes.

---

[6] There are a number of other influence statistics, including the hat matrix, studentized residuals, COVRATIO, and DFFITS. DFBETA is used here, because it shows the direct affect each applicant has on the racial coefficient estimate.

4. Matched Pairs

The fourth strategy is matched-pair analysis, which has been a standard tool used during fair lending exams for many years. Using a set of main drivers of price as matching variables, matches are identified for both minority and white applicants. For minority applicants, a white applicant is deemed a match if he or she has a worse risk profile based on the matching variables, but paid a lower price. Similarly, for white applicants, a minority applicant is deemed a match if he or she has a worse risk profile based on the matching variables, but paid a lower price. Minority and white applicants with at least one match are flagged as outliers.

The key to this strategy is determining which variables to use as matching variables. This could potentially be difficult for pricing analyses, because time and location are two important drivers of price. Unless the volume of loans is very large, it will be difficult to find matches based on time and location, as well as other measures of creditworthiness. For this study, three sets of matching variables are used. The first contains only LTV; the second adds loan purpose (refinance vs. purchase), product (fixed rate vs. ARM), and channel (retail vs. wholesale); and the third adds loan amount, income, funds available to close, and predicted price.

Unlike the other five strategies analyzed in this study, the matched pair strategy cannot be used to rank order the applicants from those most likely to be disadvantaged to those least likely to be disadvantaged. What it provides is the number of applicants with matches, which in turn defines the size of the file review sample. The number of applicants with matches falls as the number of matching variables is increased, so the file review sample size can be determined to some extent. However, it is not possible to determine how the strategy performs for all different file review sample sizes as can be done with the other strategies.

5. Forward Searching

The fifth outlier identification strategy follows Chambers *et al.* (2004) and follows the basic premise that outliers should not be included in the statistical analysis used to identify outliers. The estimates from a statistical model based on all applications in the population are affected by any outliers in that population. In turn, this affects the identification of outliers. With the forward searching method, outliers are identified using a model based on a dataset that does not contain outliers. Forward searching describes the process used to identify this dataset.

The first step of this strategy is to identify a subset of applications that does not contain outliers. This is the crucial step in the process, because all subsequent steps depend upon this initial dataset. Using all applications in the population, OLS is used to estimate a model explaining the price applicants receive on a mortgage. APR is used as the measure of price, and race is not included as an independent variable. Using the estimates from this model, the residual for each applicant is calculated. The 50 applications with the smallest absolute residuals comprise the initial subset of data that does not contain outliers.[7] This subset is referred to as the initial clean dataset. The second step is to re-estimate the model using the clean dataset. These estimates are not affected by outliers and provide robust estimates of the true underlying relationships in

---

[7] Using 50 applications for the initial clean dataset is based on the OCC's sampling policies stating that a minimum of 50 observations is a general guideline for when to use statistical estimators.

the data.[8] The third step is to use these estimates to calculate the squared Mahalanobis distance for each of the remaining applications in the population.[9]

$$D^2_{i(m)} = (y_i - \hat{y}_{i(m)})' \hat{S}^{-1}_{(m)} (y_i - \hat{y}_{i(m)})$$

where,

y_i = price for applicant i

$\hat{y}_i$ = predicted price for applicant i from a regression model based on m applications.

$\hat{S}^{-1}_{(m)}$ = estimated covariance matrix of errors from a regression model based on m applications.

The application with the smallest squared Mahalanobis distance is viewed as the least likely of the remaining applications to be an outlier. The fourth step is to augment the previous clean dataset by the one application with the smallest squared Mahalanobis distance, and repeat steps 2-4 with this augmented clean dataset.

Chambers *et al.* (2004) suggests continuing this process until the smallest squared Mahalanobis distance is greater than a specified cutoff, or all applications in the population have been processed. In the first instance, all remaining applications are flagged as outliers. In the second, there are no outliers. Chambers et al. (2004) suggest using a cutoff equal to the $(1 - \alpha/n)$ – quantile of the χ^2 - distribution.

This study takes a slightly different approach to identifying outliers. Instead of applying a cutoff to identify outliers, the forward searching process is run through all applications in the population. The OLS residuals for the original clean dataset of 50

---

[8] If the original 50 applications are generally near the means of each of the independent variables, the fit of the model using only these 50 applications will be poor, and the estimates may not reflect the true underlying relationships in the data. To check for this possibility, the Monte Carlo simulation was re-run using an initial clean dataset containing 100 application, and 150 applications. The results were basically unchanged.

[9] The difference between the squared Mahalanobis distance and the standard Euclidean distance is that the Mahalanobis distance incorporates correlations within the data [Mahalanobis (1936)].

applications, and the squared Mahalanobis distance values for the remaining applications are then used to rank order all applicants from those most likely to be disadvantaged to those least likely. The 50 applications from the original clean dataset are always viewed as the least likely to be disadvantaged. Using this approach makes it possible to show how this strategy ranks on the two performance measures for file review samples of different sizes.

6. Tree Algorithms

The sixth outlier identification strategy is a non-parametric regression procedure.[10] The basic principal of this approach is to divide the population of applications sequentially into smaller and more homogenous nodes. A node is a subset of the population. Individual applications that may not stand out as outliers in the entire population show themselves as outliers when the comparison group is smaller and more homogenous. This approach is somewhat similar to the relative residual strategy, which is a parametric procedure.

The first step of this strategy is to identify the node with the largest heterogeneity. Heterogeneity is measured as the weighted sum of squares (WSSR), where the weights are a function of a robust inference function. Specifically, the WSSR for node k is,

$$WSSR_k = \sum_{i \in k} w_{ik} (y_i - \bar{y}_{wk})^2 \qquad (1)$$

where, y_i = price for applicant i

$\bar{y}_{wk}$ = weighted mean of price for applicants in node k

---

[10] See Chambers et al. (2004) for a detailed discussion of tree algorithms.

The weight for applicant i in node k is calculated as,

$$w_{ik} = \frac{\psi(y_i - \bar{y}_k)}{y_i - \bar{y}_k}$$ (2)

where, $\bar{y}_k$ = mean of price for applicants in node k

$$\psi(x) = x(1 - \min(1, (x)^2 / c^2))^2$$

$\psi(x)$ is the bisquare influence function, and c = 4.685.[11],[12]

The second step is to take the node with the largest heterogeneity and identify all potential sets of child nodes into which it can be split. These potential sets of child nodes are determined by applying different cutoffs to the ordered values of LTV.[13],[14] For example, to create one potential set of child nodes, all applications with LTV values below some cutoff are placed into one node, while all other applications are placed into the second node. Changing the cutoff creates a different potential set of child nodes. All possible cutoffs are used to create all potential sets of child nodes.

The third step is to identify the one set of child nodes with the smallest heterogeneity. Heterogeneity for a set of child nodes is merely the sum of the WSSR values for the two child nodes. At this point, there is one more node than at step 1,

---

[11] The bisquare inference function was proposed by Tukey [Beaton and Tukey (1974)]. See Hampel *et al.* (1986) for a thorough discussion of influence functions, including summaries of a number of specific influence functions.

[12] C is the tuning constant, which determines the robustness of the estimator to outliers and the efficiency of the estimator in the absence of outliers. A value of 4.685 produces an efficiency of 95 percent when the data are normal.

[13] Some determinant of price is needed to identify potential child nodes. This study uses LTV, because it is a standard determinant of price used by many banks.

[14] Using ordered values assumes the covariate being used in the splitting process is monotone. If the covariate is not monotone, Chambers et al. (2004) suggest that potential sets of child nodes be defined for values of the covariate sorted by their corresponding average value of the dependent variable in the node.

because the node with the largest heterogeneity identified in step 1 has been split into two nodes.

Steps 1-3 are repeated until all nodes are sufficiently homogenous, all nodes are too small to split further, or a user-specified number of nodes is reached. Each time the process reaches step 3, each application within each node has been assigned a weight based on equation 2. As nodes become increasingly homogenous, the weights for any outliers in the population will tend to zero, while the weights of non-outliers will tend to 1. Formally, an outlier is identified as an application with an average weight overall node splits that is less than some user-specified threshold. Similar to the other strategies, instead of applying a cutoff, the average weights are used to rank order all applicants from those most likely to be disadvantaged to those least likely. As a result, it is possible to show how this strategy ranks on the two performance measures for file review samples of different sizes.

IV. Monte Carlo Simulation

This section outlines the Monte Carlo simulation procedure. The main drawback of using Monte Carlo simulation is that the results necessarily depend on the underlying DGP assumptions. Because of this, I take a case study approach and use data from a specific fair lending exam previously conducted by the OCC. This dataset contains 582 approvals, 186 of which are minority applicants. The simulation process controls the frequency and severity of disadvantage that is introduced into this dataset. At a minimum, then, conclusions can be drawn with some certainty about how different outlier identification strategies would have affected this exam's results. Caution must be exercised, however, in generalizing these results and applying them to future fair lending exams.[15]

The Monte Carlo simulation process consists of eight steps.

Step 1: Set the likelihood that a given minority applicant is disadvantaged.

Step 2: Set the severity of disadvantage in basis points.

Step 3: Incorporate discrimination into the original population.[16] Using random

draws from a uniform distribution, a subset of the minority applicants are

identified as disadvantaged. White applicants always face a zero probability of

being either advantaged or disadvantaged. The APR for each disadvantaged

minority is then increased by the severity amount from step two.[17]

---

[15] As a robustness check, I also ran the Monte Carlo simulation with an APR measure constructed using the sorted predicted probabilities of denial from an underwriting model. In essence, I took the role of the lender and used first-degree price discrimination based on risk to price each applicant. The advantages of this measure of APR are that it is a solely risk-based measure, and it is certain that no applicants were disadvantaged. This is important, because I want to control the frequency and severity of disadvantage in the Monte Carlo simulation. The results using this measure of APR strongly favor the absolute and relative outlier identification strategies. This is not surprising given that the APR measure is based on a multivariate model using similar independent variables as these two strategies.

[16] I assume that the original population contains no disadvantaged applicants. As supporting evidence for this assumption, using the model specification discussed in the section on absolute residuals, the null hypothesis that the being minority has no affect on price could not be rejected at the 95 percent confidence level.

[17] The simulation was also run with the severity of disadvantage allowed to vary across minorities during a given iteration using draws from a normal distribution. This had very little effect on the results. Alternative methods for incorporating disadvantage, such as allowing whites to be disadvantaged, may alter the results.

Step4: Use the six outlier-identification strategies to find the disadvantaged minorities. Except for the matched-pair strategy, the output for each strategy is a ranking of the applications from those most likely to be disadvantaged to those least likely to be disadvantaged. This ranking includes both minority and white applicants even though only minority applicants can be disadvantaged.[18] Files to review would come from those identified as most likely to be disadvantaged. Constructing the output in this manner shows how each strategy performs at each possible sample size. The actual number of files reviewed depends on available resources, evidence of fair lending risk from other components of the exam, and confidence in the approach used to identify the disadvantaged applicants.

The matched pair strategy identifies a file as needing review if there is another applicant of a different race that has a worse risk profile, but a lower price. An applicant is either an outlier or not. For any two outliers, or any two non-outliers, it is impossible to determine which is more likely to be a disadvantaged applicant. Therefore, it is impossible to create a relative ranking of the applicants. Instead, only the number of applicants identified as outliers is output.

Step 5: Construct performance measures for each outlier identification strategy. These measures are constructed using the rank-ordered output from step 4, starting with the applicants identified as most likely to have been disadvantaged. The first performance measure is the percentage of disadvantaged applicants identified at

---

[18] Both whites and minorities are included in the rank ordered lists, because during a typical exam, both white and minority applicants are reviewed to check for random inconsistency. OCC examiners do not make the assumption that only minorities are possibly disadvantaged.

each sample size. For example, suppose the current simulated population contains 10 disadvantaged applicants. If five disadvantaged applicants are identified from a file review sample size of 20, the performance measure is 50 percent. Strategies with percentages that quickly converge to 100 percent are preferred. The second performance measure is the percentage of applications in the file review sample that are not outliers. For example, if 15 of the first 20 applicants on the rank-ordered list are not disadvantaged applicants, the performance measure is 75 percent. Lower percentages indicate that resources are not being wasted reviewing applicants that are not disadvantaged. Because these performance measures are constructed for each file review sample size, each outlier identification strategy, except the matched pair approach, has two streams of performance measures. The matched pair approach has only three performance measure values.

Step 6: Execute 100 iterations of steps 3 through 5. For each iteration, the specific subset of minorities that are disadvantaged is varied based on draws from a uniform distribution described in step 3. At the end of these 100 iterations, there will be 100 streams of both performance measures for five of the six strategies, and 100 values of both performance measures for the matched pair approach.

Step 7: For each outlier identification strategy, compute the average of the performance results across the 100 iterations.

Step 8: Re-run steps 1 through 7 using different likelihood and severity values. The likelihood values analyzed during the simulation include 5%, 25%, 50%, 75%, and 95%. The severity values analyzed include 5, 12.5, 25, 37.5, 50, 62.5, 75, 87.5, 100, 200, and 300 basis points. These likelihood and severity values were chosen to provide a broad coverage of all possible scenarios. With five possible likelihood values, and 11 possible severity values, 55 total likelihood/severity scenarios exist.

V. Monte Carlo Simulation Results

This section presents the simulation results for each of the six outlier identification strategies. There are two performance measures for each of the 55 likelihood/severity scenarios, so the volume of results is large. Because of this, results are only presented for the following scenarios: 5/12.5, 5/100, 5/300, 95/12.5, 95/100 and 95/300. These results convey the main overall findings from the Monte Carlo simulation.[19] Both performance measures are presented in graphical form with a success rate and inefficiency rate graph for each likelihood/severity scenario.

Success Rate

Graphs 1a – 6a show the success rate graphs. These graphs convey how well each strategy performs at identifying disadvantaged applicants. For each of these graphs, the horizontal axis shows all possible sizes for the file review sample, and the vertical axis shows the average percentage of disadvantaged files included in the file review sample. Therefore, for a given outlier identification strategy, and a given sample size, the

---

[19] A full set of results is available from the author upon request.

graph shows the average percentage of disadvantaged minorities that have been identified for review. Strategies with higher percentages, and percentages that converge faster to 100 percent are preferable. For comparison purposes, a line is also presented, which shows the optimal scenario of the minority disadvantaged applicants all at the beginning of a list of applicants rank ordered by their likelihood of being disadvantaged.

As an example, look at the results in graph 5a. With a likelihood rate of 95 percent, approximately 177 of the 186 minorities in the simulated population are disadvantaged for each of the 100 iterations. The optimal strategy identifies these 177 applicants first. Therefore, the optimal line shows that the percentage of disadvantaged applicants found converges straight to 100 percent by a file review sample size of 177, and equals 100 percent for all remaining sample sizes. Among the six outlier identification strategies, the forward searching strategy shows the poorest performance. For a file review sample of 100 applicants, an average of only 35.4 (20 percent) of the 177 disadvantaged minorities were found. This compares with the optimal scenario in which all 100 applicants are disadvantaged for a percentage of 56.5 (100/177). Almost the entire population of 582 applicants must be included in the file review sample before all 177 of the disadvantaged applicants are reviewed. As previously noted, a stream of sample-size results is not available for the matched pair strategy. Instead, the graph shows that matching only on LTV yields an average file review sample size of 475 applicants with 161 (91 percent) of the disadvantaged applicants found on average. Similarly, using the larger set of matching variables yields an average file review sample size of 297 applicants with 108 (61 percent) of the disadvantaged applicants found on average. Finally, using the largest set of matching variables yields an average file review sample size of 107 applicants with 41 (23 percent) of the disadvantaged applicants found on average.

There are a number of interesting findings from the Monte Carlo simulation. First, no strategy appears optimal across different likelihood and severity levels. Graphs 1a and 4a show that for low severity levels, the DFBETA strategy performs best for small file review sample sizes, while the tree algorithm performs best for larger sample sizes. The switch occurs between 120 and 145 applications. For larger severity levels, the absolute and relative strategies begin to show better performance with the tree algorithm still performing well for larger file review sample sizes at a severity of 100 basis points and a likelihood of 95 percent. In general, the forward searching and matched pair strategies show the worst performance.

Second, as expected, there is a positive relationship between severity level and performance. When severity levels are low, all six strategies perform poorly. For example, at a file review sample size of 100 applicants, graph 1a shows that, on average, between 1.35 (15 percent) and 3.42 (38 percent) of the nine disadvantaged applicants had been identified depending on the outlier identification strategy used. As severity levels increase, performance improves as well as shown by graphs 3a and 6a. With a severity level of 300 basis points and a likelihood of 5 percent, five of the strategies had identified, on average, at least 8 of the nine 9 disadvantaged applicants by a file review sample size of 100.

Third, there appears to be no relationship between likelihood of disadvantage and performance. This relationship is a little difficult to see in graphs 1a-6a, because the denominators for the percentages shown in the graphs differ. When the likelihood equals

5 percent the denominator is approximately 9, and when the likelihood equals 95 percent the denominator is approximately 177. With this in mind, for small severity levels, the success rates are generally low for both likelihood values. As previously noted, the success rates increase as the severity levels increase, but they appear to increase at similar rates for both likelihood values.

Fourth, except for the extreme cases where the severity of disadvantage is large, none of the strategies are highly successful at identifying disadvantaged applicants. For example, when the likelihood is 5 percent and the severity is 12.5 basis points, on average, between 3.78 (41 percent) and 5.67 (63 percent) of the nine disadvantaged applicants had been identified for samples of 250 applicants. When the likelihood is 95 percent and the severity is 100 basis points, on average, between 83.17 (43 percent) and 141.6 (80 percent) of the 177 disadvantaged applicants had been identified for samples of 250 applicants. Interestingly, for a severity level of 12.5, all six strategies perform about as well as a simple random draw of outliers, which would be indicated by a straight line connecting the two ends of the optimal line. Based on these results, a large file review sample size is therefore typically needed for any of the strategies to identify a large percentage of the disadvantaged applicants.

Finally, the number of files needing to be reviewed to draw reliable conclusions varies greatly by the severity of disadvantage. At low levels, significantly more files must be reviewed to identify most of the disadvantaged applicants. The level of severity is not known during an exam, so other information, such as the results from the statistical analysis, should be used as signals of the severity level to help determine the

Graph 1a: Success Rate at Finding Disadvantaged Applicants

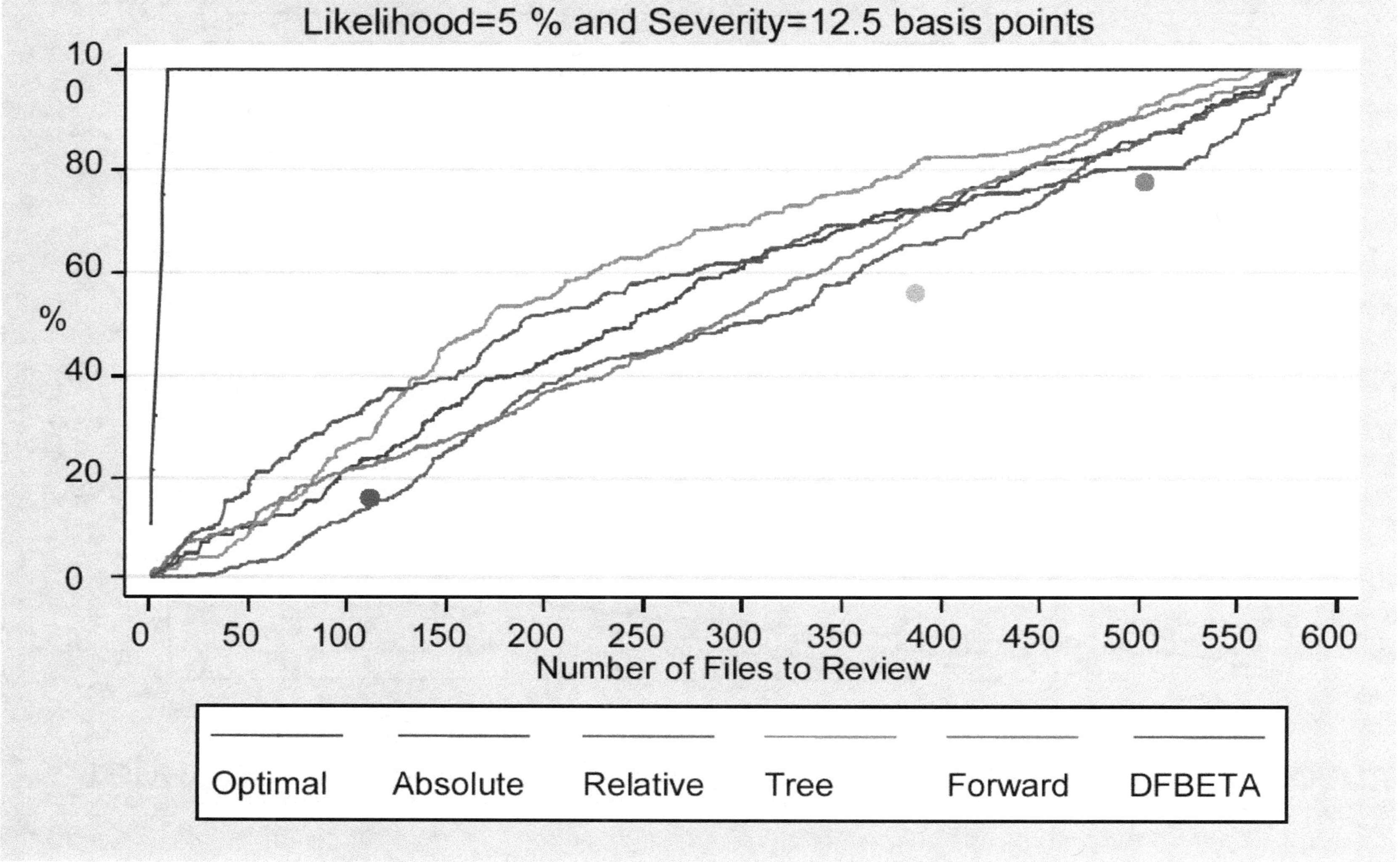
Likelihood=5 % and Severity=12.5 basis points
10
0
80
60
%
40
20
0
0
50
100
150
200
250
300
350
400
450
500
550
600
Number of Files to Review
Optimal
Absolute
Relative
Tree
Forward
DFBETA

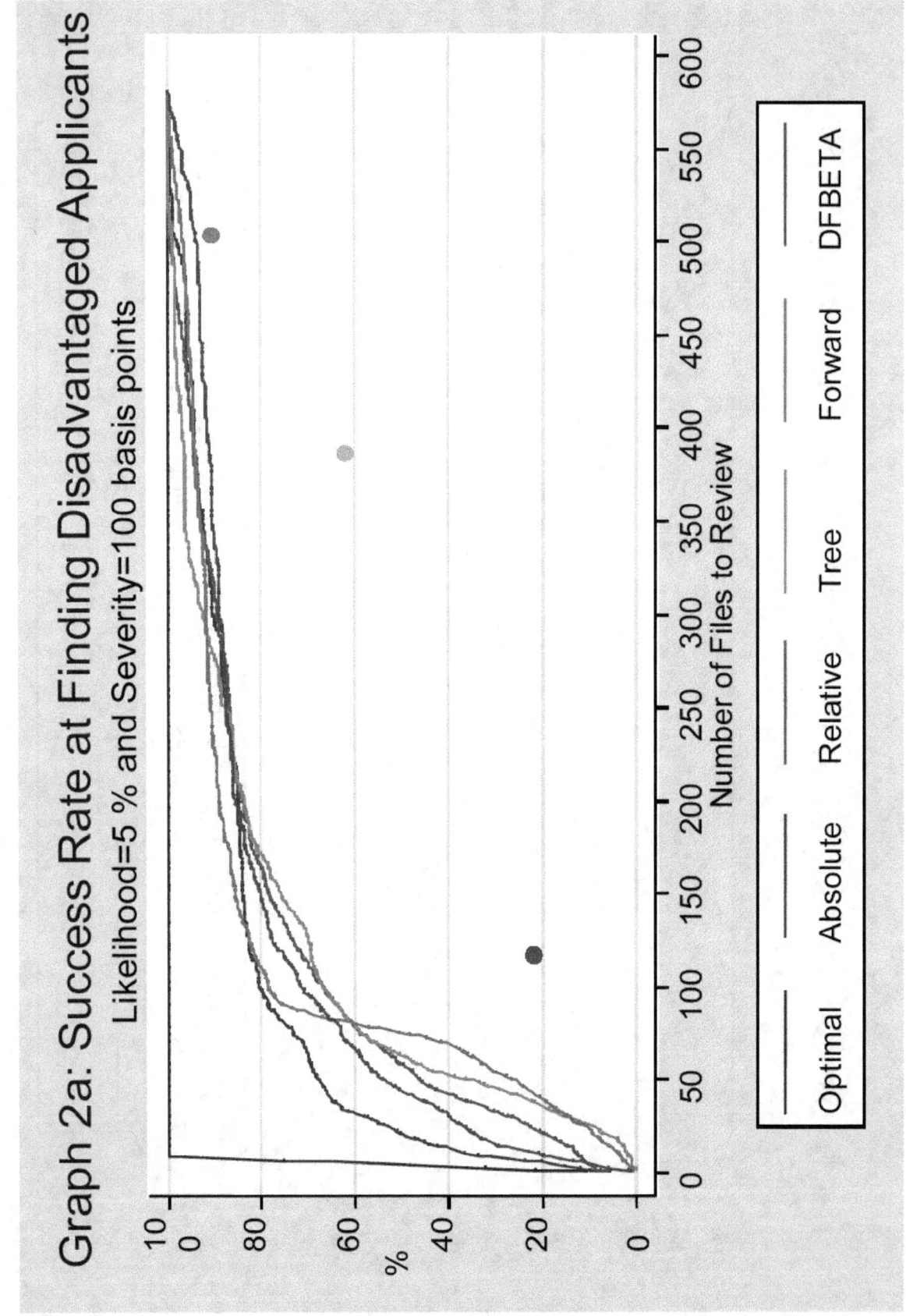

Graph 2a: Success Rate at Finding Disadvantaged Applicants
Likelihood=5 % and Severity=100 basis points

Optimal   Absolute   Relative   Tree   Forward   DFBETA

Number of Files to Review

%

24

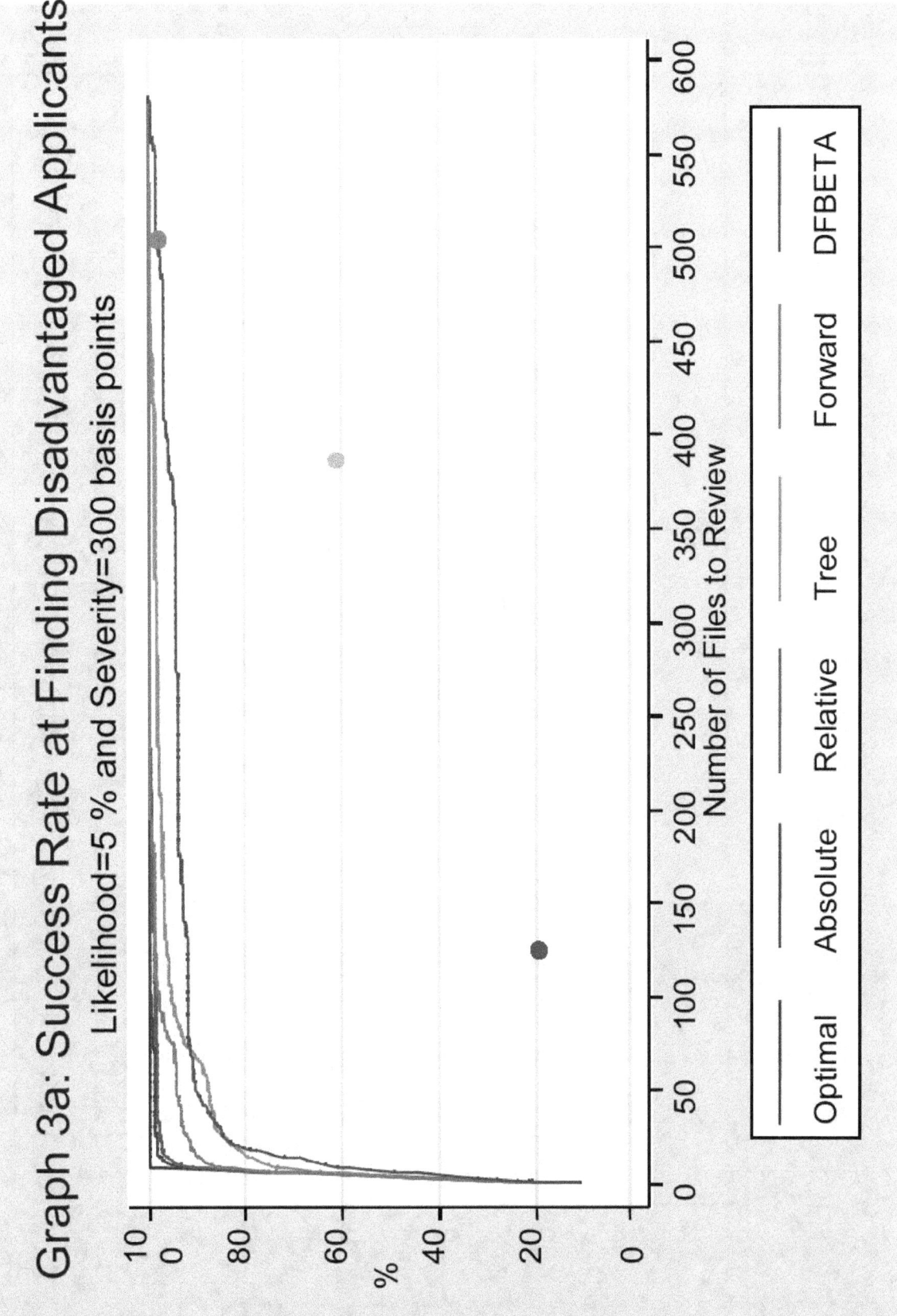

Graph 3a: Success Rate at Finding Disadvantaged Applicants
Likelihood=5 % and Severity=300 basis points

Number of Files to Review

%

Optimal   Absolute   Relative   Tree   Forward   DFBETA

25

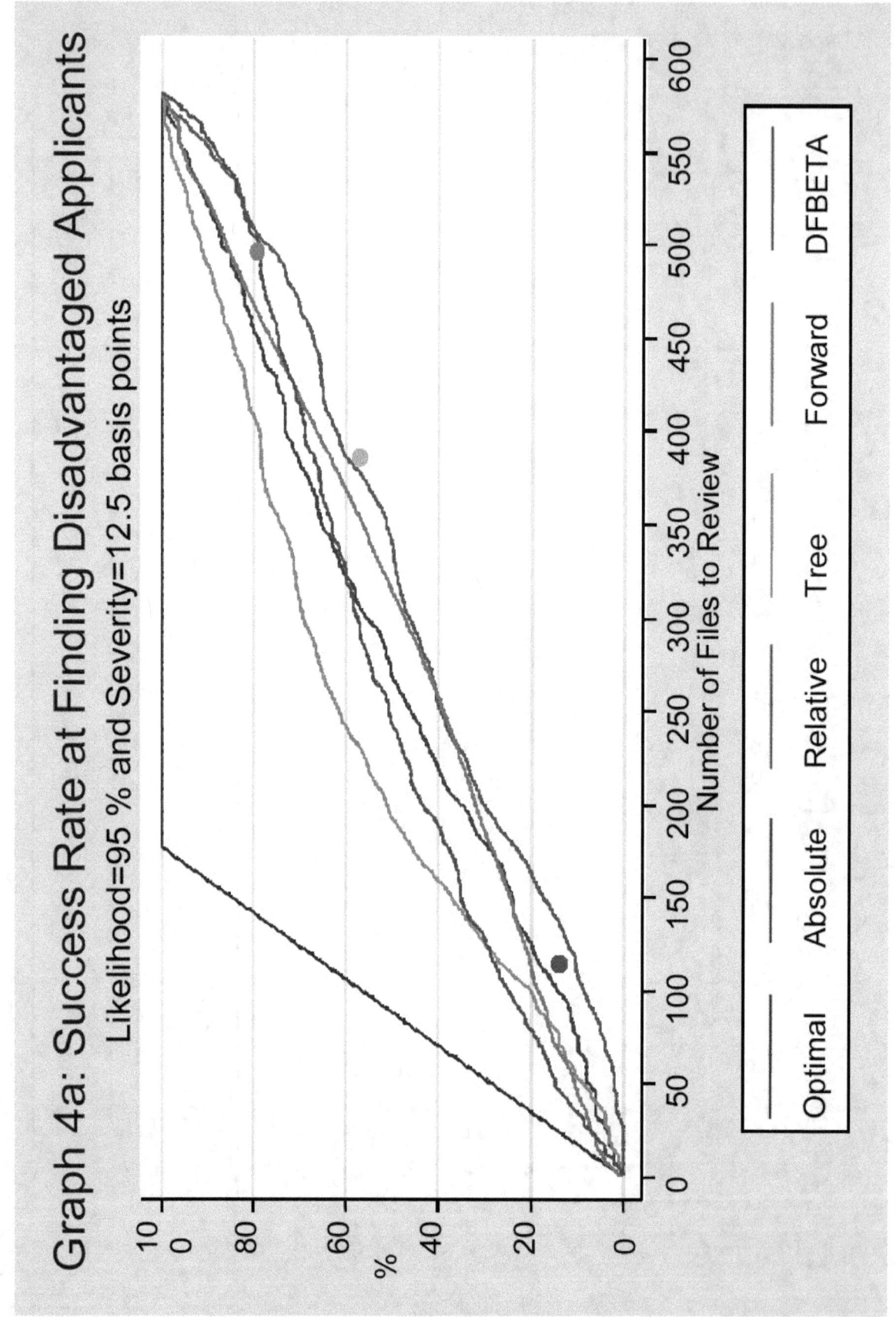

Graph 4a: Success Rate at Finding Disadvantaged Applicants
Likelihood=95 % and Severity=12.5 basis points

%

Number of Files to Review

Optimal — Absolute — Relative — Tree — Forward — DFBETA

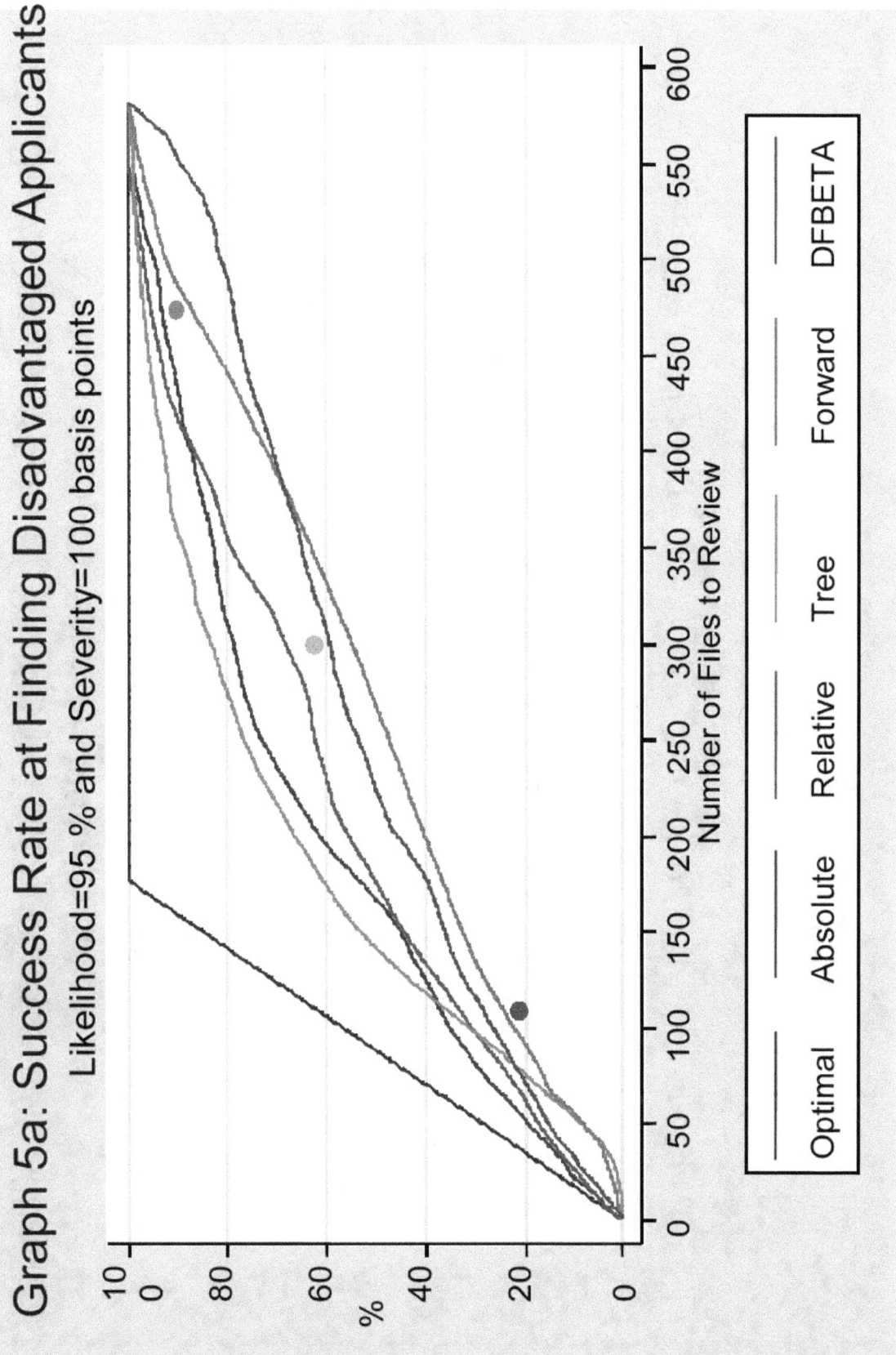

Graph 5a: Success Rate at Finding Disadvantaged Applicants
Likelihood=95 % and Severity=100 basis points

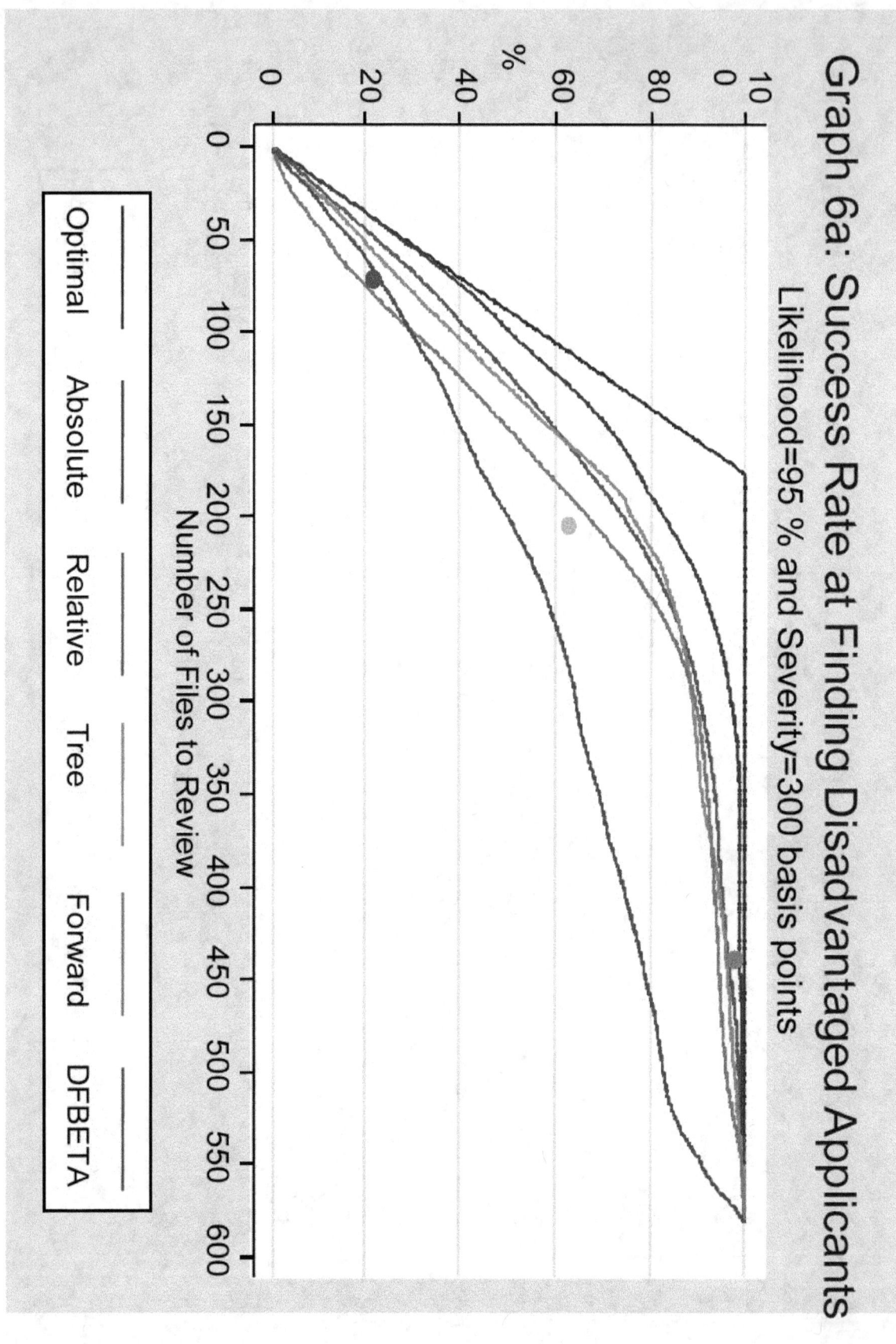

Graph 6a: Success Rate at Finding Disadvantaged Applicants

Likelihood=95 % and Severity=300 basis points

%

Number of Files to Review

Optimal — Absolute — Relative — Tree — Forward — DFBETA

appropriate sample size. For example, if the statistical results suggest potential discrimination, a larger sample of files should be reviewed.

Inefficiency Rate

Graphs 1b and 2b show the inefficiency rate graphs. Only two graphs are presented, because the success rate graphs contain much of the same information as the inefficiency graphs. For a given file review sample size, as the success rate at finding disadvantaged applicants increases, the percentage of applicants reviewed who are not disadvantaged decreases. Therefore, the success and inefficiency rate graphs mirror one another. The primary reason for presenting the inefficiency graphs is to convey more directly the degree of inefficiency; something the success rate graphs do not show well. For example, suppose for a given file review sample size that a strategy identifies 50 percent of the disadvantaged applicants. To determine the inefficiency rate, the total number of disadvantaged applicants must be known. This information can be determined from the success rate graphs by multiplying the likelihood percent by 186, the total number of minorities in the population. However, this is a poor method for conveying inefficiency rates.

For both of the inefficiency rate graphs, the horizontal axis shows all possible sizes for the file review sample, and the vertical axis shows the average percentage of files that are not disadvantaged minorities. Therefore, for a given outlier identification strategy, and a given sample size, the graph shows the average percentage of files in the file review sample that are not disadvantaged. This is a measure of inefficiency and wasted resources. Strategies with lower percentages are preferable. Again, for comparison purposes, a line is presented, which shows the optimal scenario of the minority disadvantaged applicants all being identified first, followed by all other files.

As an example, look at the results in graph 1b. With a likelihood rate of 95 percent, approximately 177 of the 186 minorities in the simulated population are disadvantaged for each of the 100 iterations. The optimal strategy identifies these 177 applicants first. Therefore, the optimal line shows that for file review samples with 177 or fewer applications, the average percentage of applicants who are not disadvantaged in these samples equals zero. After a sample size of 177, all subsequent applicants are not disadvantaged, so the optimal line converges to 68.04 percent, which is the total number of applicants not disadvantaged divided by the total population size of 582. Compared with the optimal case, each of the outlier identification strategies result in a large percentage of the file review sample consisting of applicants who were not disadvantaged. For a file review sample of 50 applicants, the average number of applicants who were not disadvantaged ranged from 24 (48 percent) for the DFBETA strategy to 45.0 (90 percent) for the Relative strategy. This suggests considerable resource waste as files are being reviewed that need not be reviewed.

The primary finding from the inefficiency rate graphs is that a large number of applicants not disadvantaged were identified by each of the outlier identification strategies. This suggests significant drain of resources as these files are unnecessarily reviewed. Looking at graph 1b, which shows inefficiency rates for a likelihood of 5 percent and a severity of 100 basis points, except for small file review sample sizes, the percentage of the sample consisting of non-disadvantaged applicants is above 80

30

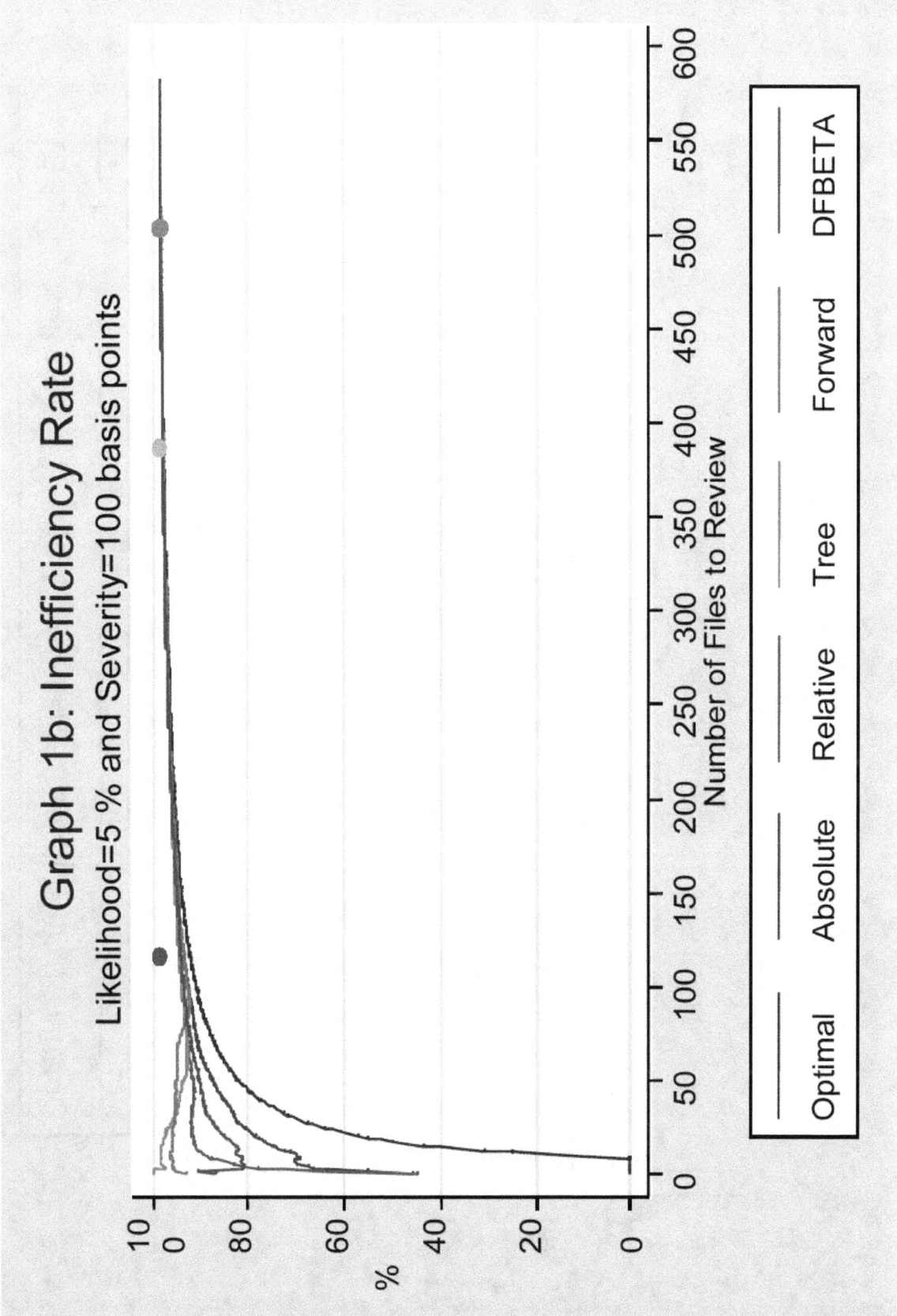

Graph 1b: Inefficiency Rate

Likelihood=5 % and Severity=100 basis points

Number of Files to Review

%

Optimal   Absolute   Relative   Tree   Forward   DFBETA

31

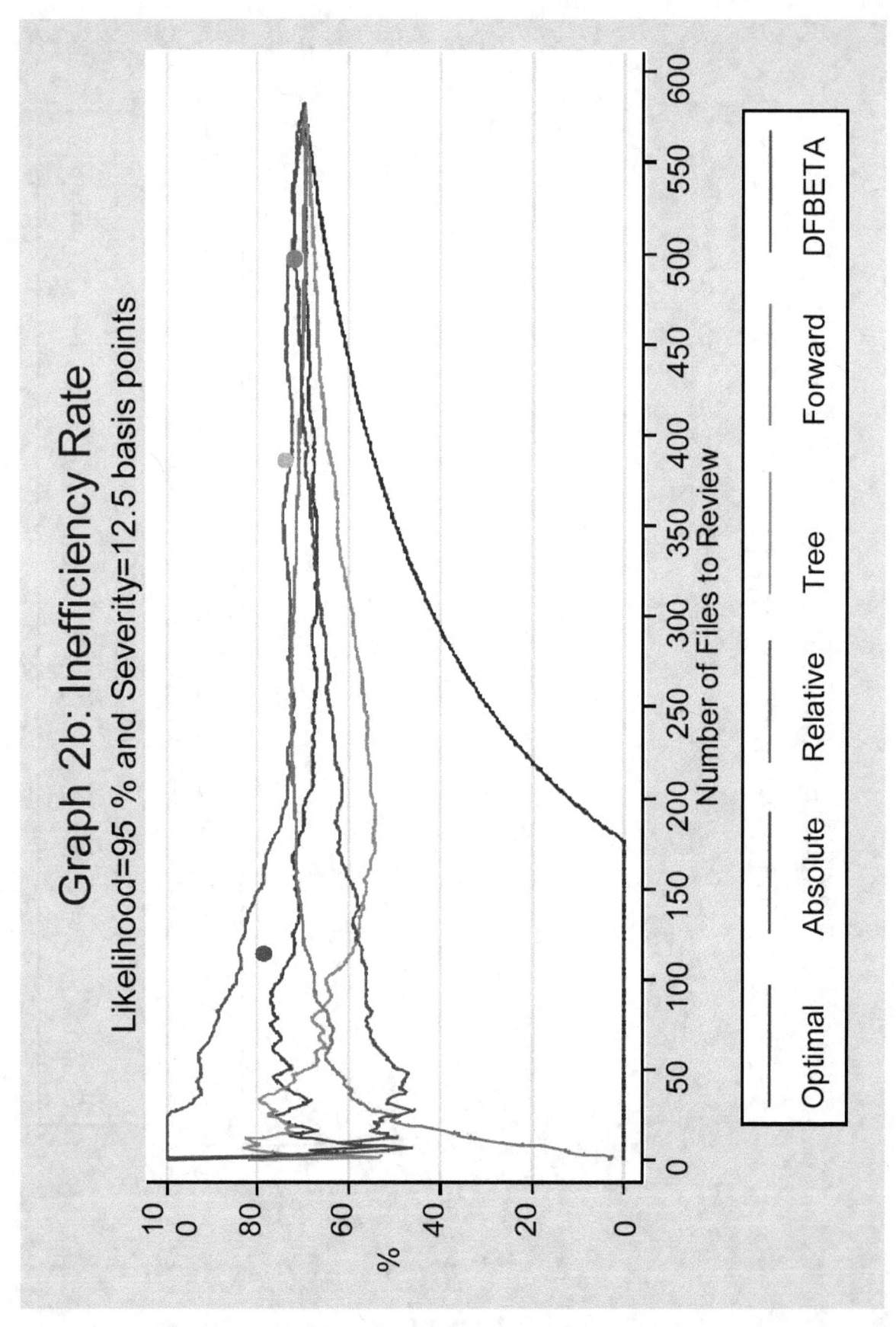

Graph 2b: Inefficiency Rate
Likelihood=95 % and Severity=12.5 basis points

Number of Files to Review

%

Optimal   Absolute   Relative   Tree   Forward   DFBETA

32

percent. Graph 1b shows lower inefficiency rates, but still generally above 50 percent for all file review sample sizes.

VI. Conclusion

The file review portion of a fair lending exam provides supporting evidence to the statistical analysis and identifies disadvantaged applicants. The strategy employed to identify files for review affects the reliability of conclusions and the cost of the analysis. A preferable strategy successfully identifies disadvantaged applicants at a high rate, while minimizing the number of files that are not disadvantaged applicants. A number of strategies are available to identify files to review. However, no study has compared and contrasted the performance of those strategies to determine the strategy best suited for fair lending exams.

This study uses Monte Carlo simulation to compare the performance of six outlier identification strategies. The likelihood of being disadvantaged is varied from 5 to 95 percent, and the severity of disadvantage is varied from 12.5 to 300 basis points. Performance is measured by the success at identifying disadvantaged applicants and excluding applicants that are not disadvantaged.

Overall, no strategy revealed itself as the optimal outlier identification strategy. Depending on the likelihood/severity scenario, the DFBETA, absolute, relative, and tree algorithms all showed stronger performance. In addition, except in extreme instances, no strategy was highly successful at identifying disadvantaged applicants or minimizing those that were disadvantaged. The main message is that more work must be done to identify a strategy showing better performance. This includes exploring variations of the six approaches analyzed in this study and testing additional strategies.

Given the large volume of results, and the mixed messages of these results, it is worthwhile to conjecture which set of results might most reflect reality. In other words, which outlier identification strategy should be used for future fair lending exams? Manually reviewing files is resource intensive, so steps are typically taken to minimize the number of files reviewed. This is one of the major advantages of using statistical tools on the front end of the analysis. Manual review of more than 100-150 files implies significant resource cost. This eliminates the tree algorithm, which showed the strongest performance in larger file review samples. The forward searching and matched pair analysis strategies generally showed the weakest performance across all likelihood/severity scenarios and are ruled out from consideration as well. The DFBETA showed the strongest performance for small severity levels, while the absolute and relative strategies performed better as the severity level rose. Given that the absolute strategy has been used historically, and is likely the easiest to understand, that strategy should continue to be employed to identify outliers during future fair lending exams.

References

Atkinson, A.C. (1994) Fast Very Robust Methods for the Detection of Multiple Outliers, **Journal of the American Statistical Association**, 89:428, pp. 1329-39.

Barnett, V., and T. Lewis. (1978) Outliers in Statistical Data, Chichester, England: John Wiley.

Beaton, A.E. and J.W. Tukey (1974) The Fitting of Power Series, Meaning Polynomials, Illustrated on Band-spectroscopic Data, **Technometrics** 16, pp.147-85.

Chambers, Ray, and Adao Hentges and Xinqiang Zhao. (2004) Robust Automatic Methods for Outlier and Error Detection, **Journal of the Royal Statistical Society**, 167, part 2, pp. 323-39.

Hadi, Ali S. (1992) Identifying Multiple Outliers in Multivariate Data, **Journal of the Royal Statistical Society**, 54:3, pp. 761-71.

Hampel, F.R., E.M. Ronchetti, P.J. Rousseeuw, and W.A. Stahel (1986) Robust Statistics: The Approach Based on Influence Functions, New York:Wiley.

Hawkins, Douglas M., and Dan Bradu. (1984) Location of Several Outliers in Multiple-Regression Data Using Elemental Sets, **Technometrics**, 26:3, pp. 197-208.

Mahalanobis, P.C. (1936). On the Generalized Distance in Statistics, **Proceedings of the National Institute of Science of India**, 12, pp.49-55.

Maronna, Ricardo A., and Victor J. Yohai. (1995) The Behavior of the Stahel-Donoho Robust Multivariate Estimator, **Journal of the American Statistical Association**, 90:429, pp. 330-41.

Pearson, E.S., and C. C. Sekar. (1936) The Efficiency of Statistical Tools and a Criterion of Rejection of Outlying Observations, **Biometrika**, 28, pp. 308-19.

Rocke, David M., and David L. Woodruff (1996) Identification of Outliers in

Multivariate Data, **Journal of the American Statistical Association**, 91:435, pp.

1047-61.

Appendix A: Data Descriptions and Summary Statistics

Table A1: Description of Variables Used in Analysis		
Variable	Description	Excluded category
Noterate	Note rate	--
Retail	Retail channel	Wholesale channel
Refi	Refinance loan	Purchase loans
Fixrate	Fixed rate loan	ARMs
Jumbo	Jumbo loan	Conforming loans
Size	Loan amount	--
Cntycat1	Group of counties*	All other counties
Cntycat2	Group of counties	All other counties
Cntycat3	Group of counties	All other counties
Cntycat4	Group of counties	All other counties
Cntycat5	Group of counties	All other counties
Spclpgm	Special pricing program	Regular pricing
Male	Male	Females
Nohs	Neither primary nor co-applicant has more than a high school diploma	Other education levels
College	Either primary or co-applicant has college degree	Other education levels
Edumiss	Education data missing	Other education levels
Finoccup	Job is related to finance	Job unrelated to finance
Selfemp	Self employed	Not self-employed
Income	Income	--
Ownerocc	Owner occupied	Not owner-occupied
Tottrade	Total number of trade lines	--
Fndtocls	Funds to close	--
Msnum	Market share number	--
Msvol	Market share volume	--
Numbanks	Number of lenders in tract	--
Fatal	Applicant has a fatal characteristic	Not fatal
Dumhdti	Housing DTI is above policy cutoff	
Dumdti	Back-end DTI is above policy cutoff	
Ltvcomb	CLTV	--
Insufund	Insufficient funds to close	Sufficient funds to close
Score1	Custom credit score	--
Score2	Custom credit score	--
Score3	Custom credit score	--
Rapid	Rapid processing of application	Not rapid application
Frsttime	First time home buyer	Not 1st time buyer
Minority	Black or Hispanic	White
* For confidentiality reasons, the specific counties comprising each group cannot be revealed.		

Table A2: Summary Statistics of Population (582 approved applications)				
Variable	Mean	St. deviation	Minimum	Maximum
Noterate	7.06	1.19	5.00	9.09
Retail	0.57	0.49	0	1
Refi	0.39	0.49	0	1
Fixrate	0.56	0.50	0	1
Jumbo	0.26	0.44	0	1
Size	162.27	66.92	16	300
Cntycat1	0.20	0.40	0	1
Cntycat2	0.20	0.40	0	1
Cntycat3	0.25	0.43	0	1
Cntycat4	0.09	0.28	0	1
Cntycat5	0.08	0.27	0	1
Spclpgm	0.26	0.44	0	1
Male	0.85	0.36	0	1
Nohs	0.12	0.33	0	1
College	0.56	0.50	0	1
Edumiss	0.07	0.25	0	1
Finoccup	0.05	0.22	0	1
Selfemp	0.11	0.32	0	1
Income	74.35	47.08	12	530
Ownerocc	0.94	0.23	0	1
Tottrade	25.55	15.05	1	84
Fndtocls	48,786.07	181,323.29	-143,005.00	3,269,006
Msnum	7.28	4.08	0	27.83
Msvol	5.77	4.16	0	39.46
Numbanks	89.14	34.04	25	219
Fatal	0.02	0.37	0	1
Dumhdti	0.27	0.44	0	1
Dumdti	0.38	0.49	0	1
Ltvcomb	81.38	16.37	9.90	102
Insufund	0.17	0.37	0	1
Score1	2.91	22.09	0	498
Score2	0.81	5.87	0	102
Score3	0.11	1.32	0	30
Rapid	0.25	0.43	0	1
Frsttime	0.32	0.47	0	1
Minority	0.32	0.47	0	1